The Hedge Organisation

A STORY TO SHOW HOW PEOPLE CAN BECOME LOST IN THE CORPORATE HEDGE

Paul Williams

Grosvenor House
Publishing Limited

Paul Williams is hereby identified as author of this
work in accordance with Section 77 of the Copyright, Designs
and Patents Act 1988

The book cover picture is copyright to Paul Williams

This book is published by
Grosvenor House Publishing Ltd
28-30 High Street, Guildford, Surrey, GU1 3HY.
www.grosvenorhousepublishing.co.uk

A CIP record for this book
is available from the British Library

ISBN 978-1-78623-026-3

CONTENTS

THE STORY BEHIND THE STORY

This is the story of Mike Ramsey – a good, decent man who starts his own company.

After a promising beginning the company expands, but unfortunately its financial fortunes gradually wane and Mike faces financial ruin.

The reason for the company's decline is that Mike's management team gradually lose focus, they misuse their positive personality traits, and also become diverted by non-value-adding activities. All of these problems are more likely to occur in large companies where there are more opportunities to become distracted, whereas smaller organisations have to remain completely focused in order to survive.

Eventually Mike realises that his company has become like an out of control hedge, and in order to regain control he has to show true, genuine, authentic and inspirational leadership if he is to reverse the company's financial fortunes.

I hope you will find the story that guides this book interesting, useful and even entertaining. On the front cover you will see an illustration of Mike's management team lost in the corporate hedge, and you might wonder why there's no illustration of Mike himself; this is because he might well be someone you know – or maybe even you!

THE STORY

The Beginning

Mike Ramsey had just moved into 45 Acacia Avenue in Windall with his wife and 2.5 children (he used this joke at dinner parties as there was a baby on the way). It was a pleasant, leafy avenue, evenly lined on either side with mature flowering cherry trees.

He had left his old widget company in Teeford, where he had been the production manager, to start his own widget company. Mike knew all about widgets, and in fact at his old company people had often referred to him as the widget king, a title he had accepted and worn with modest pride.

Having secured the finance for his new venture, using his house as security, Mike was busy overseeing the refurbishment of an old factory so that it would become a "state-of-the-art" widget production facility. The work all went according to Mike's plan; little wonder, as Mike was a fastidious planner, precise and accurate, but never too ambitious. All his life Mike had used these skills to steadily climb

Windall Widget Company

MD: Mike Ramsey

the corporate ladder, rising from maintenance fitter to production manager.

But now things were different, or as Mike liked to put it, this was the time for a paradigm shift in his life. He wasn't quite sure what the word "paradigm" meant, but he had heard it mentioned in a lecture on organisational change at Teeford Technical College in one of the optional modules he had selected as part of his HNC in mechanical engineering. However, he was sure it was something to do with radical change – and that was the journey Mike was now on.

Another thing Mike was proud of was that several of his old colleagues had, although perhaps a little jealous of his ambitious plans to start his own company, given him a leaving present of a book entitled "Entrepreneurial Skills". However, when reflecting on this kind gift, Mike wasn't quite sure if the message behind it was that he already had, or maybe needed, to acquire these skills.

Within six months the new factory was ready. Mike was very proud to walk around it and view the new manufacturing equipment, the prestigious although not too extravagant offices, and the newly land-scaped grounds, complete with a water feature just outside the oak front door. And what Mike was particularly proud of was the new sign at the entrance: "Windall Widget Company - MD: Mike Ramsey"

He wasn't sure if he should have a parking space for himself, as he had read in an article on employee engagement in "Widget Weekly" that it could be seen as elitist, and that was one thing Mike certainly wasn't, so as a compromise he simply put a sign on the space nearest the front door which said "Reserved". Mike thought that as no-one would know who it was reserved for he could make use of it himself.

To mark the completion of the factory, Mike thought it would be a good idea to plant something in the garden of his new home, so he could see both his business and his garden flourish at the same time. Not wanting to plant something that had no purpose, as this wouldn't complement the growth plans he had for his business, he wanted to plant something that was both ornate and useful. He dwelt on the matter for a few days, a process Mike often utilised: as he would frequently say when dealing with issues, "Let me sleep on it". After several nights, Mike arrived at the perfect thing to plant: a hedge in the front garden. This would be both pleasing to the eye and useful. And, as there was no front wall it would prevent people from encroaching onto his garden and possibly peering into his bay window, something he thought was quite likely, as the number 19 bus to the centre of Windall stopped right outside his house. Not that he really minded, as he felt this had been adequately reflected in the purchase price of the house he had finally negotiated with the estate agent.

So, as the business grew he could then see his hedge grow too, and he would nurture and care for them both.

The Recruitment Process

Having planted the hedge over one weekend – Mike was never a person to drag a job out once he had made a decision – he turned his attention to recruiting the team he would need to manage and run the factory. From his previous experience Mike knew all the key positions which he identified as:-

- Marketing
- Sales
- Production
- Health & Safety
- Finance
- Human Resources (HR)

He was thinking of having a legal department, but felt that these services might best be provided on an "as required" basis by WB Foster, a local firm of solicitors who had been recommended to him by Major Prendergast-Smythe, who was the chairman of the Windall Chamber of Commerce. Mike had joined the Chamber of Commerce when he first moved into the area as he felt it would enhance his position, and coincidentally as it turned out, Major Prendergast-Smythe was the chairman of WB Foster!

Mike settled down to write detailed job descriptions for each post that included comprehensive roles and responsibilities.

Mike was so pleased with his final draft that he had it bound into a book and the spine inscribed with "Windall Widget Company Department Heads, Roles & Responsibilities". He placed it on his new mahogany bookshelf in his not too large office, next to his other book, "Entrepreneurial Skills". Glancing casually but rather proudly at the two books, he decided they weren't quite sufficient for a managing director, but he thought he could soon solve this problem by visiting his local book shop at the week-end and acquiring a few more books on suitable topics, such as leadership, performance management, and whatever other impressive tomes in the business section would support, and even enhance, his new image.

Mike decided he would recruit all the heads of department himself, and that they in turn could then recruit their own teams. Mike felt that this was fair, and it supported his view that he needed to empower people – again something he had learned on another optional leadership module of his HNC whilst at Teeford Technical College. Empowerment was something that rang true with Mike, as he had been empowered by his own ex-managing director; although he had wondered whether his MD's daily visits and weekly reporting requirements had been full empowerment, or rather "empowerment with reservations".

Although he felt quite capable of doing it himself, to support the recruitment process Mike decided it would be a good idea to apply some personality profiling techniques, such as the Belbin Team Role Assessment and Insights Discovery tool, two techniques that he himself had once completed on a team awayday. Although he hadn't completely understood the roles that had been assigned to him from these exercises, Mike had felt comforted by the fact that the Belbin analysis had identified him as a strong team player, and Insights had described him as an earth green. These he felt described him perfectly, as he saw himself as a truly "down to earth, supportive person".

Mike hired Weaver and Wiltshire, a local firm of headhunters, to help with the recruitment process. They were again recommended to him by Major Prendergast-Smythe from the Chamber of Commerce, who Mike found out later was coincidentally also its chairman!

So adverts were placed online, in national papers and in trade magazines, including what Mike thought was probably the best source for recruiting the right people, "Widgets Weekly". Mike had often contributed to the publication himself, not so much as an author of articles, but by submitting lengthy letters to the "Opinions" page – although none had ever been published. However this didn't deter Mike, as he kept all his letters in a folder so that he could proudly show them to factory visitors.

Interviews were arranged for all the heads of department, and each candidate was given a one-hour screening interview by the consultants, together with personality-profiling assessments, and then a short-list of four people for each post was interviewed by Mike and the lead consultant, for final selection. Mike felt that this process was sufficiently robust to both identify suitable candidates and also satisfied his own desire for thoroughness.

After three months, all the department heads had been selected. There was Colin, head of finance, with impeccable qualifications, who had made a slow yet steady rise up the corporate ladder from a junior invoicing clerk in a local firm of estate agents, to head of accounts for a building society. He seemed polite and capable, and Mike particularly liked his deliberate and precise style. As he said to the consultant who had advised him to appoint a more ambitious and energetic candidate, Colin was just what he needed: someone to steady the ship in times of trouble – not that Mike envisaged there would be any troubles, but he always felt it was best to be prepared "just in case". And his appointment also satisfied one of Mike's often used mantras, "Hope for the best, but prepare for the worst".

Then there was Pete, head of marketing. Mike was particularly impressed by Pete's education – private school then university. This was in sharp contrast to Mike's education at the local comprehensive and technical college. And what particularly won Mike over was Pete's smart attire of pin-striped suit, pink shirt and floral tie, and to top it all off golf club cufflinks. That said it all to Mike, and made up for Pete's career history, which did seem rather erratic, with often no longer than six months at any one company. But still, Mike thought, this showed desire and ambition, which he felt his new fledgling organisation could readily satisfy.

The role of head of HR was filled by Tina. Simply suffice to say that Mike found her enthusiasm, energy and passion truly engaging. She was also into social media. Mike had read about this in many newspaper articles, and it was a communication trend he thought should definitely be embraced by both himself and his new company.

Tina also seemed very interested in Mike's plans for the company and asked so many questions, not only about the company, but also about Mike's family and interests, that the interview overran by 45 minutes!

The appointment of the production manager posed more of a problem for Mike, mainly because this was his own domain and it was going to be difficult for him to find someone who could live up to his own high expectations and standards. Eventually he settled on Jim, who quite frankly took Mike's breath away, not only by his obvious vast experience in both hands-on and management positions in manufacturing, but also with his natural quick wit and humour. In fact he couldn't stop Jim from telling a few anecdotes which were very amusing, and Mike knew that his sense of humour would energise a team.

Sarah took the position of head of sales, and what a whirlwind of energy she was. She had so many contacts, both inside the industry (she had worked for another widget company for over five years), and even more outside of work, where she knew so many people from the numerous clubs and societies to which she belonged. And what also intrigued Mike was that she kept mentioning all the parties and events she had either been to, or had planned in the future – a real socialite!

Finally came health and safety, and eventually Mike settled on Nigel, who was obviously demanding as he had mentioned at the interview a whole catalogue of issues he had encountered over the years, not only in his own function but also in many others, but which he assured Mike he wouldn't allow to occur in the Windall Widget Company! He particularly impressed upon Mike the need to always understand what the root cause of any problem was rather than just the symptoms, and also to never accept what anyone said at face value, but delve for any hidden personal agendas.

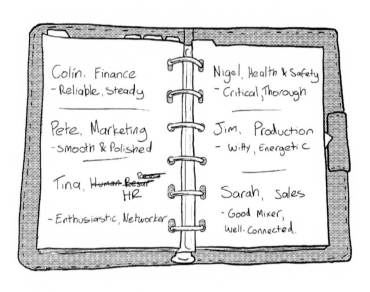

So there it was, the team was now complete, and as he mused over them he saw how their skills were not only perfect for their roles, but also complementary – something the consultant had said had been verified by their personality profiling results.

In fact, Mike was so pleased with the people he had selected he thought he would write their names and corresponding skills down in a page in the new Filofax he had recently bought (he preferred a Filofax to the complexity of an iPad).

As Mike went home that night, after the last position had finally been filled, and he approached his own house, he couldn't help noticing that the hedge he had planted a few months ago was growing nicely, and that the gaps between each individual bush had closed.

His hedge, like his team, was now complete.

The Good Times

When the factory was ready it was opened and the ribbon cut by the Chairman of the local Round Table, another organisation Mike had joined, as he felt this one would help him to make some prestigious contacts in the local area; although he had been somewhat deflated when one evening his wife had pointed out that she thought it was highly unlikely that anyone in the Round Table would either need, or want to buy widgets! Mike dwelt on what he thought was a rather unhelpful comment, but dismissed it, as he thought to himself that all contacts would lead to new contacts, and that these new contacts might well indeed need to buy some widgets.

As the months turned into years the company, like his hedge, grew, and Mike often reflected on the similarity between them both. The company and the hedge, created and planted at the same time, were flourishing, and both were giving Mike satisfaction. The company provided him with status in the local community, where he was now vice-president of the Windall Trade Association. It was affiliated to the Chamber of Commerce, to which he still belonged, but as there didn't appear to be an opening for high office in the Chamber of Commerce or the Round Table he had switched his focus and attention to the Trade Association instead, and in any event the vice president's position there gave him a ceremonial chain of which he was particularly proud. His hedge also gave him satisfaction because, like his company, it symbolised strong, permanent and continual growth.

Widgets were selling well, and the company was growing in size. As Mike had left the daily running of the factory to his heads of department, this had left him with the time and space to make plans for the future, and to also involve himself in a wide variety of networking activities.

He had joined the local golf club and he now played there regularly; he had even taken a few weeks off for an intensive course of lessons. Mike had also enrolled in a half-day-per-week French language course, as he knew that the Windall Widget Company would soon be going international, and he felt that the MD should be in the vanguard and lead the way in being able to speak at least one other language. He had chosen French as the language to study, not because the French had any more passion or desire for widgets than any other country, but as Mike had taken (although failed) a GCSE in French at school he was sure this would give him a head start. He had also privately thought to himself that as soon as the company started exporting he could add the word "International" to the sign at the front entrance – something that would give him deep pride, pleasure and personal satisfaction.

With all his new plans and activities, Mike had had little time to spare to look after his garden at home, and one day noticed that the hedge was beginning to become somewhat overgrown. As he left for work one morning, after waving goodbye to his wife, he wryly thought to himself as he closed the wrought iron gates and climbed into his top-of-the-range Ford Mondeo that the company was becoming much like his hedge – gradually larger, and also a little difficult to control!

In the first five years, widget sales steadily increased – so much so that the Windall Widget Company was making substantial annual profits, and Mike was persuaded by Sarah from sales to throw a celebratory party. Mike thought this was a good idea, and Jim from production offered to do an amusing after dinner speech. Mike wasn't sure if it was wholly appropriate for one of his heads of department to act as a stand-up comedian, a view that was reinforced by Nigel from health and safety, and who had also passed the comment that it wasn't the only inappropriate thing going on in the company. Mike didn't want to continue this slightly negative conversation, but dwelt on the fact that Jim was turning into a comedian, and that Nigel was becoming a little over-critical on a number of issues.

The party went well, but as Mike drove home that night (he never drank alcohol at any business event, a tip he had been given by his old MD, who had said, "Never let your guard down and alcohol can destroy it") he thought that some of the departmental heads' attitudes had changed. Sarah had seemed to spend an inordinate amount of time at work organising the party, and although Jim's after-dinner speech had been funny, he appeared to be morphing into something of a clown, and Nigel was becoming hyper-critical.

However, Mike had been buoyed by the comment made by Pete from marketing, who said that he thought the evening had been a great success, and that Mike himself had come across at the party as engaging and inclusive. Mike felt somewhat comforted by this, although he had found it a little unnerving that Pete always seemed to be at his side during both the pre and post-dinner drinks, and had also sat next to him at the dinner – strange!

The Decline

As time rolled by the celebration party became a distant memory – as did profits.

Over the next few years the company continued to grow both in terms of employees and turnover, but profits gradually went in the opposite direction; eventually the company was turning in annual losses and its future was in jeopardy!

One evening, after leaving the office late, Mike wearily drove back home, and he paused and stood to look at the hedge he had so optimistically planted when he first started the company all those years ago. The hedge was now completely overgrown and well over seven feet high! It was darkening his house and annoying his neighbours, and its thickly knotted and entwined branches were out of control – just like the Windall Widget Company!

In fact, he thought to himself, my company has become "The Hedge Organisation"!

Reflecting and pondering on the problems of his hedge-like organisation, Mike reluctantly decided that radical action was needed – something that was at variance with his usual steady and exacting natural tendencies. He had been faced with similar situations before, and knew when enough was enough: maintaining the status quo would lead to failure. There wasn't even time to sleep on it!

It was like the time he had been a scout master for the 2nd Teeford troop, when during one camping weekend the camp fire wouldn't light with traditional sticks and matches, and he had taken the decision to send the senior patrol leader down to the local Co-op store for some firelighters. Mike had thought at the time that this wasn't admitting defeat, but simply taking practical steps to overcome an apparently insurmountable problem – something he had to do now!

But what to do as far as his hedge organisation was concerned? What would sharpen the team up? What would get them focused? What would bring them together? What would encourage them to work as one united team?

Mike had noticed over the last year or so how each department had seemed to develop into individual fiefdoms. Each had become so insular that at department heads meetings people seemed to spend more and more time blaming their own poor performance on other groups – and no-one ever offered to help anyone else. It appeared that members of each department increasingly seemed to drift around the site as individual groups, like swarms of bees, or even worse, marauding enemies.

So what would bring them together? Mike mulled it over in his office at home one evening after dinner, having sat through an episode of *Eastenders* with his wife – which, with all its associated arguments and despair, he couldn't help thinking shared many similarities with his own organisation – he suddenly had what Mike called a "light bulb" moment; the answer, he thought, was staring him in the face!

He again repeated the question he had asked himself. "What would help build the department heads into a better team?" It was obvious – a team building event! That was the answer. He would get to work and arrange it the next day. He was full of anticipation and excitement, certain that a really well-organised team building event was just what was needed.

So, the next day he discussed the idea at his morning management meeting, and whilst it didn't exactly receive enthusiastic endorsement, at least everyone agreed to take part, and Sarah from sales offered to organise it.

The event took place a few weeks later over two days at Windall Adventure Centre, and involved a whole range of outdoor activities, including go-karting, clay pigeon shooting, archery, and even an assault course; the exercises were also interwoven with classroom activities to identify and deal with the issues that were preventing them from working together as one cohesive and effective team.

The event was facilitated by Watsons of West Windall, a company Mike had read about in "The

Windall Weekly", and who had run a series of team building events for Windall Wanderers, the local football team who played in South West Division 4. According to the article, the Wanderers were destined to rise up the league following Watsons team building events, however, on checking the league table Mike was a little disappointed to find the team languishing in the bottom half of the league. Still, he thought to himself that maybe before the team building event they had been even lower.

Mike was eagerly anticipating the event, but the two days were a complete disaster. The competitive activities were used to settle scores, and the classroom sessions to cast aspersions on each other's personalities, suggestions and views. In fact Jim summed the situation up quite succinctly during one session on working together and said, "Let's face it, offsite events are usually a waste of time, because if you're a cantankerous negative idiot at work you'll be a cantankerous, negative idiot when clay pigeon shooting" which Mike thought could have been a sideways snipe at Nigel?

So when they returned to work after the team building event they had learnt little, if anything, and were certainly no more closely bonded together. In fact, things seemed to be even worse!

The Search For Help

Following the debacle of the team-building event, Mike let the dust settle, but things still weren't improving, so he decided to explain the problem to Major Prendergast-Smythe over after-dinner drinks at a Chamber of Commerce event one evening, having listened to a talk by a local retailer on customer care. The Major gave his advice with his usual confidence and panache, although Mike was slightly perturbed by the skewed angle of the Major's bow-tie, his more than usually flushed face, and his rather claret-tinged moustache.

The Major assured Mike he was well-versed in matters of efficiency, and advised him that, rather than concentrate efforts on building his management into one team, what he needed at this time was a "simplification manager". Someone who would strip out all the unnecessary processes and procedures, leaving Mike with a lean and efficient company – or, as the Major stridently put it, a "Lean, mean, fighting machine". Mike had read about lean organisations in an issue of "Strategic Management" (a publication he had recently subscribed to, as he had heard that it was one of the most influential publications in the business world) and thought it was a good idea, so he readily agreed to the Major's suggestion.

The Major recommended someone called Simon from Penfold and Pegasus, who he said had vast experience in dealing with similar situations, and although the Major was not directly connected to the company, he did mention that his brother-in-law was the major shareholder.

Mike met Simon the following week at the golf club where Mike was now well-known to the bar staff, as since the downturn in the financial fortunes of his company he spent more time in the bar than on the course. As a simplification manager, Simon seemed to have all the right credentials: he was smart, debonair and confident, and talked fluently about his many triumphs and successes, but what really impressed Mike was that he passed favourable comment on Mike's newly acquired golf club cufflinks.

Later that week, encouraged by the conversation with Simon, Mike decided to do something about his hedge and purchased a new hedge trimmer. He was heartened by a certain similarity between Simon and his state-of-the-art trimmer – both definitely looked the part, had a certain elegance, and although they were also rather expensive, he felt they would do a sterling job.

So Simon set to work, grilling each department head: how many people they had, how they were organised, what were each team members' roles and responsibilities, and what were the supporting processes and procedures.

Armed with all this information, Simon embarked on something he explained to Mike was a "Brown Paper Exercise". Mike felt he had understood the concept, although he was somewhat surprised when he entered the room assigned to Simon to see that he actually was using brown paper. He had stuck it around all four walls and had begun to populate it with activities, deliverables and accountabilities. Mike wondered why the paper had to be brown, as he personally would have preferred white, since it would have seemed much cleaner and brighter.

After a month had passed, Simon seemed to be making little, if any, progress. Each department head robustly defended their staffing levels, explaining in great detail the critical role each person played, and many warned Simon that taking anyone away would jeopardise the operation of the entire company.

Jim from production had been particularly robust in the defence of his department, and emphasised to Simon that if he removed any one of his staff the company would come crashing down like a pack of cards. As Simon went on, since he knew relatively little about exactly the way the company worked, he found he couldn't counter the department heads' defensive positions.

Eventually, Simon presented Mike with his findings and said that, although he was an experienced simplification manager, to do justice to the project, given the obvious complexity of the interwoven processes and procedures (and Mike's mind briefly flashed back to his knotted and intertwined hedge at home) he would need to create a simplification team and bring in five other consultants to help him.

That weekend, as Mike reflected on Simon's proposal to tackle his out of control company, he decided it would be an appropriate time to tackle his out of control hedge. Armed with his smart new hedge trimmer he toiled to get the hedge back under control, and after an afternoon's hard work stood back to admire his handiwork. But he was disappointed to see that he had only managed to trim the outer branches, and although it looked slightly neater, the hedge was essentially still much the same. Rather like his heads of department, who had thwarted Simon's attempts to thin out their operations, his hedge had also shown similar resistance to his own efforts. It had become impregnable and resistant to change – just like his company.

After attending a Sunday service at his local church, where the sermon had been on partnership building between the church and the local community, he dwelt on the problems not only of his hedge but, more importantly, those of his "hedge organisation". Team building had been a disaster, and tackling the processes and procedures of his company hadn't worked either. Perhaps the problem didn't lie with the team dynamics, or the processes and procedures, but instead with the individuals' attitudes and behaviours. Had he given his departmental heads too much freedom and autonomy? Had he abdicated responsibility? Had he shown true leadership?

The selection process had been very thorough, and he knew his department heads had all the right personal attributes, but maybe now they had lost focus and were applying them in the wrong way.

Slightly dejected, but also strengthened by thinking that maybe the individuals were the key to reversing the company's financial fortunes, rather than how they worked together, or the processes themselves, he delved into his Filofax and found the page on which he had written the departmental heads' attributes and positive behavioural traits after the interviews all those years ago.

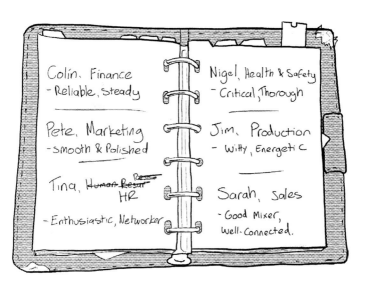

Colin, Finance
- Reliable, Steady

Pete, Marketing
- Smooth & Polished

Tina, ~~Human Resou~~ Resour
HR
- Enthusiastic, Networker

Nigel, Health & Safety
- Critical, Thorough

Jim, Production
- Witty, Energetic

Sarah, Sales
- Good Mixer,
  Well-Connected.

He had seen Colin from finance as steady and reliable, but his steadiness had developed into "just doing enough". Yes, he couldn't fault the accuracy of the accounts, but Colin offered no fresh ideas for reducing costs, or introducing new ways of working. He came in on time and left on time – to the minute. Yes, he attended all the team meetings, but never offered any ideas, and just went along with everything and everybody. He was simply just doing enough. He had morphed into Colin the Coaster.

Mike had seen Pete, the head of marketing, as polished, smooth, smart, hard-working and diligent. Pete continually stayed late, although he did recall what Nigel had said about Pete leaving soon after Mike. Nigel had also passed the comment that Pete always went quiet when Mike left the room, but was then the first to speak again when he re-entered. These two comments now began to gain some resonance. Mike thought that Pete always said the right things at the right time, and always supported Mike's views. He was the first to respond to Mike's emails, and was always available for a conversation or meeting at any time. In fact, Pete had even rung Mike when he was on holiday with some ideas he had been thinking about. The more Mike thought about it, the more he realised that Pete made presentations and comments on other people's work, but produced little material himself.

He talked well, and always looked good – he had become Pete the Politician.

Gradually, as Mike made his way down the list, he realised that he had allowed everyone's positive behavioural traits to drift and become misdirected so that they were no longer adding value to the company's objectives.

He had once seen Tina as enthusiastic, but her enthusiasm seemed to involve everyone in everything she did. She would also send copious emails and continually ask people to explain to her what they were doing. Everything revolved around Tina. Her enthusiasm wasn't so much contagious as suffocating. Mike realised that Tina had become a Time-Stealer.

Mike then turned his thoughts to Jim, the head of production, whom he had originally thought of as his rock and a kindred spirit, given that he was performing the function closest to Mike's heart, and who he had perceived as engaging and witty. Jim had at first used his wit to energise people, but as time went by he spent more and more time just "being funny". He would joke at every opportunity, be it at team meetings or offsite events. He would interrupt, and punctuate serious and important conversations, with what he saw as witty retorts and remarks. He would continually search for, and email, funny stories and jokes, and he would roam the factory armed with his latest store of amusing ammunition – he had become Jim the Joker.

As he went through the rest of his department heads with the same critical assessment, Mike broke out into a cold sweat. His hands became sticky, and his pulse began to race.

Mike had seen Sarah from sales as a good mixer, but all she did now was drift around the company socialising. She spent the whole time flitting from person to person, or group to group, engaging everyone in idle conversations. She had become Sarah the Social Butterfly.

Finally, he thought about Nigel from health and safety. He had seen Nigel as intellectually critical, but his critical eye had gradually become more and more cynical, negative and sarcastic. He saw the bad in everyone and everything. He had become Nigel the Negative Cynic.

So there it was. As he gazed down, mesmerised by the Filofax list that he had optimistically penned all those years ago, he scribbled what they had become next to each person's name.

Not only were people using what Mike had originally perceived as positive behavioural traits in a negative way, and hence adding no value to the business, the internal company processes and procedures had proliferated. Layer upon layer of new company standards and ways of working had become overly-complex and were stifling real efficiency and strangling the company; they were as inter-twined as the branches of his hedge in his front garden at home.

The plethora of processes and procedures had been accompanied by what Mike saw as an exponential growth in the number of meetings and emails. He couldn't help but notice that all his department heads seemed to be having meetings after meetings, with some overlapping, which resulted in them often running down the corridor from one to the other. And when they weren't engaged in meetings, the little time they did have free seemed to be taken up with emails.

Mike wasn't even sure whether the meetings were adding any value, and was reminded of what his old MD had often said about meetings not being work, but about deciding what to do. He had also said that when you send an unnecessary email to anyone you are stealing someone's time. Mike's concern was exacerbated when he looked at the department heads' open calendars and noticed there appeared to be a growing trend for having pre-meetings, agenda meetings, the meetings themselves, action-allocation meetings, and post-review meetings. Mike also noticed that, when sending emails, everyone seemed to be copying them to everyone else.

And meetings and emails weren't the only activities that were proliferating. People had started social and sporting clubs during the working day, so much so that after waiting in reception for 15 minutes one of his visitors had amusingly but rather disturbingly remarked that people seemed to be arriving with so much sporting paraphernalia that for a moment his guest had thought he was in a David Lloyd leisure club!

Mike also became aware that numerous other activities were being spawned which didn't seem to add much, if any, value to the company's core objectives; there were the occupational health visits for good posture and back pain, attendance at networking events, and the painting competition – which he noticed some people were completing their entries for during the working day!

Yes, the company had, like his hedge at home, grown out of control. Team building hadn't worked, simplification hadn't worked, so now he had to do something else – but what?

He pondered on the problem, searching for a solution one Sunday afternoon as he drank another glass of whisky in an effort to block out the looming return to work on Monday. As more alcohol was consumed, Mike reflected that he used to look forward to Mondays when the company had been in its infancy. He would literally run into work, smile at the company sign, and rush up the stairs to his office (although he never actually ran upstairs, or took two stairs at a time, as this was strictly against the company's safety policy and reinforced by Nigel's stairway code.) Now he had to drag himself into work and, when leaving his house in the morning, he would slowly trudge down the path and not even glance at his out of control hedge, as he knew it would remind him of where he was heading – to his out of control company.

Mike would climb into his aging Ford Focus (he had downsized from his top of the range Mondeo, as cash was now a real issue) and slowly make his way into work. And the Ford Focus wasn't the only cost saving measure Mike had been forced to take as the annual losses began to mount. There were no more team nights out. No more golf days. He had even sent an email out to instruct his team that before any meeting they had to call the facilities co-ordinator to let her know how many people were attending so that she could allocate one biscuit per person.

Not only was Mike having to make these drastic cost saving measures in order to survive, he was also being pursued by the bank, who had provided an overdraft facility for working capital which, like the original start-up loan, was secured on his house in Acacia Avenue. But now, on seeing the rather obvious downturn in the fortunes of the Windall Widget Company, the bank had asked for the overdraft to be repaid in full, and had passed the matter on to their debt recovery team. Mike felt that this was somewhat heavy-handed – a feeling reinforced by what he saw as the very noticeable change in attitude. The original bank manager had been so friendly, amiable and even warm, and always called him Mike, whereas the debt recovery people were brusque, officious and cold, and always addressed him as Mr. Ramsey in a rather stern and slightly threatening manner.

So, after a few more hours pondering in his office, and a few more whiskies (which Mike knew was rather foolish on a Sunday afternoon, although somehow seemed necessary), he decided to get some fresh air and mow the back lawn. He preferred to work in the back garden now so that he could avoid looking at the front hedge, which only served to remind him of his company's problems. Whilst slowly pushing his lawnmower up and down to leave neat stripes in the lawn, which somehow bought some transient calm to his troubled mind, his obvious anxiety was clearly etched on his hollowed face (he had lost almost two stones in the last few months), and it was noticed by his neighbour, Frank, who, after some pleasantries, enquired if everything was OK.

Although Mike was a proud and private man, he was at the point when he felt the need to unburden himself to someone, and quickly summarised the problems he was encountering with his company to Frank. Frank listened intently, and once Mike had finished he said he knew someone who might be able to help. Mike's mind immediately flashed back to the other offers of help he had received over the years – the recruitment consultant, Major Prendergast-Smythe at the Chamber of Commerce, Simon the Simplifier – and he stiffened as Frank explained that he had a friend called Tony at the rugby club they both supported, who was a lecturer at the Windall Management College, specialising in organisational development. Frank went on to say that he would be happy to effect an introduction to see if Tony might be of any help and, more out of desperation and despair than hope, Mike agreed.

The following week Mike met Tony at the Plough pub in the centre of Windall. Tony had seemed very amiable on the phone when they had spoken to arrange the meeting, and Mike had been particularly buoyed and encouraged by Tony's positive and confident tone and manner, attributes that had been eroded from Mike's personality with his company's decline.

Over a few pints of real ale at the Plough, which took Mike back to happier days at the Swan and Duck close to Teeford Technical College, he carefully, precisely and accurately outlined the history of the Windall Widget Company to Tony. Although he omitted to mention the similarities between his ailing company and his garden hedge, it was constantly swirling around in the back of Mike's mind during the conversation. Like Frank, Tony listened attentively, something Mike put down to them both being interested in rugby, a sport which required attention, dedication and discipline.

This unburdening process – for that is what it was – lasted for over two and a half hours. Mike was drained, but Tony remained genuinely engaged and interested.

Tony supped the last of his pint, which Mike quickly replenished, and he then started to provide an analysis of the situation Mike's company was in. Tony said that Mike's planning and setting up of the company had been thorough; he had sourced the right equipment, and selected experienced and competent staff. The issue was that as a company grows it provides the opportunity for people to become distracted. He explained that everyone has positive personality traits, easily identifiable by various personality profiling techniques, but the issue was how they applied them. Tony continued, and explained about something he called "behavioural drift" so, for example, a person who is naturally creative can use their creativity to either generate and propose new ideas for improving the efficiency of the organisation, or use it in a negative way to identify the flaws in other people's views, ideas and opinions. Mike's mind flashed to how hyper-critical Nigel had become; although Mike had seen his positive personality traits as being thorough and critical at the interview, Nigel was clearly now using these traits in a negative way.

Tony carried on by saying that even if people do not use their positive traits in a negative way they can, if given too much freedom, overuse them and disturb and distract other people (and Mike immediately thought of Jim, who had overused his natural wit, and Sarah her sociability).

Tony then went on to say that, given the opportunity, people can also drift into getting involved in non value-adding activities, and Mike quickly thought of all the unnecessary emails, meetings and social events, and how his visitor had mentioned that the reception area resembled a leisure club.

Finally, Tony mentioned that as a company grows so does its processes and procedures and that, if allowed to proliferate without any periodic review and appropriate adjustment, they can ultimately stifle and suffocate it, and not easily be untangled by someone who doesn't have a full understanding of the organisation.

Mike remained silent for a while after Tony's analysis, and it gradually dawned on him that Tony had uncannily and accurately described exactly what had happened to his company. It had become a hedge-like organisation, and the people were lost in it.

To break the silence, and also to ease the pain clearly etched on Mike's drawn and ashen face, Tony continued by offering some sage guidance and advice to help Mike plan a way forward. He explained that what was required was to refocus people and ensure that they used their personality traits positively, and concentrated on value-adding activities which supported what the business was trying to achieve.

This required strong inspirational leadership, and privately Mike ruefully thought about all the peripheral activities that he himself had become involved with; the golf club, French lessons, and various networking activities – and he had even contemplated standing for election as a local councillor. He had set up and administered the company, but had not followed this through with true leadership. He had not only taken his eye off the ball, he couldn't even see it now as it too, like his staff, had become lost in the hedge!

Tony continued by explaining that in order to help people remain focused on value-adding activities, individual, team and company targets should be set, displayed and reviewed. It was what Tony explained was a combination of effective performance management and the creation of a powerful visual organisation, both of which would energise people so that they could see the positive effect their efforts were having on the company's performance.

He also said Mike should parallel this by taking a keen interest in what people were doing so that they felt their efforts were valued and then, if appropriate, Mike could acknowledge and celebrate them, something Tony called positive reinforcement.

Finally Tony summarised by explaining that as companies grow and experience organisational difficulties, all too often leaders focus their efforts on dealing with processes rather people issues, however he assured Mike that if he refocused people's personality traits on supporting the business the unnecessary processes, procedures and activities would gradually and naturally fade away.

This all made perfect sense to Mike, and he thanked Tony profusely for his insightful analysis and sound advice.

That evening, as Mike walked slowly back from the Plough and up his front path, he took a sideways glance at his hedge and smiled, and then sat quietly in his study and dwelt on the evening's conversation. Tony was right, his entire team had lost focus and had used their positive personality traits not to support the business, but instead had drifted into negative or over-used behaviours and non value-adding activities, and he himself had also become equally as distracted and not shown true leadership.

But things would change, and as a start he decided to shut himself away in his office at home listing each department heads' behaviours in his Filofax so that he could have one-to-one conversations with each of them the following Friday to realign and refocus them to support the business. And this is how the conversations went.

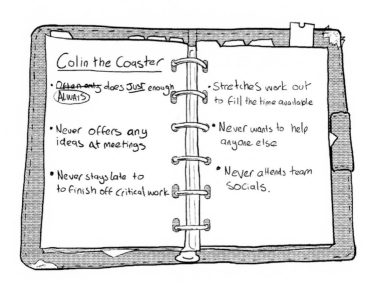

The Conversations

Colin The Coaster

The first meeting was with Colin and, having carefully provided him with a summary of his behaviour, it came as something of a shock to Mike that he didn't seem at all surprised or defensive! He even agreed with Mike's analysis, and seemed almost resigned to its authenticity. Colin agreed that he had drifted into just doing enough and had become detached not only from his peer group, but also from his team and even the company. His coasting had cast him adrift.

Mike went on to explain how his steady style could benefit the team, as it could provide balance, continuity and substance; he just needed his steadiness to be accompanied by a desire to look for opportunities for efficiency improvements in his own function and, where appropriate, offer assistance to others.

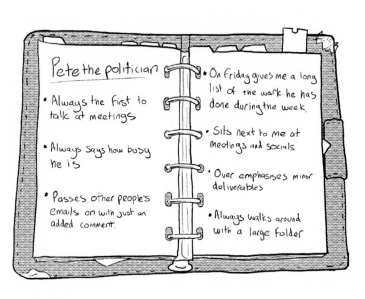

Pete the politician

- Always the first to talk at meetings

- Always says how busy he is

- Passes other people's emails on with just an added comment.

- On Friday gives me a long list of the work he has done during the week.

- Sits next to me at meetings and socials

- Over emphasises minor deliverables

- Always walks around with a large folder

Pete The Politician

Mike thought he would start this conversation on a positive note and asked how Liverpool football club, Pete's favourite team, were performing in the premiership. Pete immediately said they were currently 5th in the league, and with 3 easy games left and a points difference of over 30, would probably qualify for Europe next year.

Trying to move the conversation on to a business footing, Mike asked Pete what he thought about the last quarterly production figures. Pete thought for a moment, and then had to admit he wasn't quite sure, but thought they hadn't been too good. Mike quickly and painfully reflected that Pete seemed to know all about the performance of Liverpool football club, but little about the company that provided him with the funds to pay to watch them!

Mike then moved on to Pete's feedback, which Pete initially received with an air of indignant surprise and instantly started to defend his position, but gradually and somewhat reluctantly began to admit that his marketing training had taught him about the need to "always look good", but he agreed he had probably taken it too far. He had focused his efforts on trying to impress Mike rather than direct his time and energy to searching out new markets.

They then discussed how Pete's ability to make things look good could be used to positive effect in profiling the company to its clients, as long as it was accompanied by rigorous attention to his marketing role.

Tina The Time-Stealer

Mike knew that this would be a difficult and painful feedback conversation for both himself and Tina. Tina had a heart of gold – a heart she would share with anyone at any time.

During the feedback she provided not so much a defence as an explanation of her behaviour, and indicated she was only trying to help; but she had to agree that she did tend to involve other people in things too much – a trait she put down to her insecurity and a lack of confidence in her own skills and ability. Mike assured her that her ability was not in question, and that she didn't have to search out and look for affirmation from others. He explained that if Tina became more focused she would be even more effective in her role, and be able to free up time to devise and introduce new HR initiatives to motivate, focus and energise others which would, in turn, improve the performance of the company.

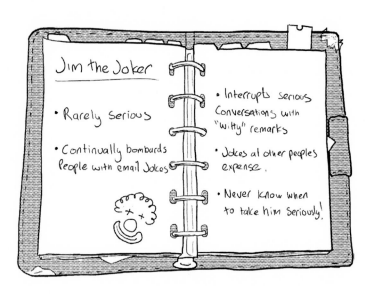

Jim the Joker

Mike explained that Jim seemed to be using work as a stage on which to perform. Yes, he could be very funny, but didn't seem to know where to draw the line in any conversation or meeting. Mike continued to explain that by joking all the time, other people couldn't take anything he said seriously.

Mike went on to suggest that Jim could use his humour and wit at the start of a meeting or in a conversation to relax people to create a harmonious atmosphere and indeed, on occasions, make humorous interjections to defuse any interpersonal friction. Humour could also, where necessary, be used to re-energise a flagging meeting, but Jim needed to use it sparingly to be effective.

Sarah the Social butterfly 🦋

- Spends most of Monday mornings regaling people with tales of what she has been up to at the weekend.

- Seems to drift around the company engaging people in social conversations

- Always arranging social events

- Continually involved with social media.

- Always planning the next holiday whilst at work.

- Spends an inordinate amount of time on her mobile phone in the corridor

- Always has a privacy screen on her computer.

Sarah The Social Butterfly

Another rather difficult conversation was with Sarah who, being head of sales, had to meet people both at work and socially to develop relationships and win orders.

Mike explained that the problem was that her innate and potentially powerful ability to make strong personal bonds with people could energise, engage and entertain them, but that it had drifted towards a more personal bias, so that she was spending too much of her time simply socialising with everyone.

Mike continued by saying that if her social skills were focused more on customers she could drastically improve the order book, and could also provide valuable help in building a strongly bonded team within the company by channelling her skills into organising occasional team building events.

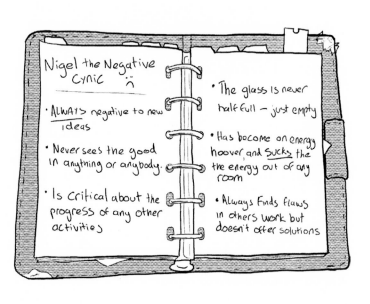

Nigel The Negative Cynic

Finally came Nigel. Mike started the conversation by telling Nigel that he had a tendency to disagree with anything anyone said. Nigel quickly retorted with "No I don't" and Mike replied with what he saw as a witty but potentially dangerous riposte: "See, you're doing it again!". Fortunately they both laughed, and continued with a mature and adult conversation.

Nigel's early defence was that he was just being an "agent provocateur" to ensure there were no flaws in any plan or activity, but he had to admit that it could be seen as hyper-critical. What had the biggest effect on Nigel was when Mike said he had become an "energy hoover" and could suck the energy out of any meeting or conversation, leaving people he interacted with as deflated balloons.

Mike went on to explain that, if used in a positive and pleasant manner, Nigel's highly logical mind could add value by identifying solutions to problems and delivering them in a positive way, but to use it in an accusatory manner all the time to highlight flaws in others work was demoralising, de-energising and demotivating.

Mike completed these discussions on the Friday as he had planned. He had chosen Friday so that his team could reflect on the conversations he had had with them over the weekend, and also so that he himself would have the time to recharge his batteries after what he knew would be a physically and mentally exhausting exercise – and it had been.

The Turnaround

When Mike returned to work on Monday morning he did so with a renewed spring in his step. He gathered his team together and reiterated the poor financial state of the company, something he had carefully discussed with each of them individually during the previous week's coaching conversations, and stressed that only if they worked together as a completely united and supportive team did the company stand a chance of survival. Mike continued by outlining the need for increased sales, a more reliable manufacturing process, and a significant reduction in operating costs.

To his surprise, amazement and delight, every member of his team became genuinely engaged in the ensuing conversation, and spontaneously offered suggestions and ideas for possible actions. Jim didn't try to steal the show with any inappropriate jokes, Tina listened intently, Colin offered ideas, Nigel built on people's suggestions, Sarah volunteered to arrange an away-day for the team to build a cohesive plan, and Pete suggested that specific targets should be set and reviewed at each weekly meeting.

The team really had changed, and for the better!

Over the next few months, as his team helped devise and implement the company's recovery plan, Mike set individual, team and company targets, took a keen interest in what each team member was doing, and had regular progress meetings both on a one-to-one and team basis. He walked the factory floor every day and reviewed every process and procedure with his team, removing those that were adding no value, so it gradually de-cluttered his tangled organisation. He introduced the visualisation that Tony had suggested, and displayed targets and progress for each team and for the company.

Gradually, formal meetings and email traffic reduced as everyone focused on adding value.

Mike had transformed himself from being the managing director of the Windall Widget Company into its inspirational leader.

As he sat at home one evening drinking a cup of tea (the whisky having been confined to social occasions now), he reflected on the reason his company had grown out of control as it had become larger – and indeed as his front garden hedge had too – and it was that he had neglected both. The staff at work had become lost in the "corporate hedge" not because they wanted to, but because they could. Now that he was showing true leadership they had transformed from coasters, politicians, time-stealers, jokers, social butterflies and negative cynics into real value-adders!

After only a year the company became profitable again, the overdraft was cleared, and he was once again returned to the care of his original friendly bank manager.

The following year Mike entered the company into a national competition, and it was awarded "Most Improved Factory of the Year", and Sarah organised a celebratory dinner.

Mike even bought a new iPad – although he did clad it in a leather case so that it reminded him of his beloved Filofax.

And yes, Mike did finally find the time and energy to tackle his hedge. He bought some protective goggles and strong secateurs, and got inside the hedge to strip out the dead wood and release the intertwined branches. He showed the same attention and diligence to his hedge as he had to his company.

Both the company and his hedge flourished, growing at the right pace, and in the right direction.

As a permanent reminder, and to make sure he didn't regress, Mike removed the "Reserved" sign from the car park and replaced it with "Visitors", and took down the "Windall Widget Company, MD Mike Ramsey" sign, and replaced it with the

Windall Widget Hedge Organisation – something he knew would need some explaining.

And Mike would be more than happy to oblige.

FINALLY

I hope you have enjoyed reading the story of Mike Ramsey and the Windall Widget Company, and have found it useful, interesting, and even amusing.

During my career in working with companies to improve operating performance and commercial profitability I have encountered a wide variety of people, almost all of whom wanted to work diligently to apply their experience, expertise and skills to support the companies they were working for.

That said, I have also met the characters described in this book: people who have lost their way. People who, given the freedom and space often associated with large organisations, have either over-used or mis-applied their positive personality traits, and also spawned a plethora of unnecessary processes, procedures and activities.

This inevitably leads to corporate inefficiencies resulting in a reduction in operating and commercial performance.

In an attempt to rectify the situation managers and leaders have a natural tendency and preference to tackle processes and procedures rather than people issues. This focus can not only be ineffective, it can actually exacerbate the situation and create further inefficiencies. What is required is to ensure that people's behaviours, attributes and skills are applied positively to support the company's objectives through true and genuine leadership.

Everyone wants to work hard and add value in order to gain and sustain their own self-esteem – it's just that without strong, authentic and inspirational leadership they sometimes get distracted, and become lost in the corporate hedge.

If this book has stimulated you to want to know more about the issues raised, or how to build excellence into a company, please contact admin@wcg.uk.com

Lightning Source UK Ltd.
Milton Keynes UK
UKOW02f1811070716

277906UK00001B/1/P